SALES::

How to Sell, Influence People, Persuade and Close the Sale

CONTENTS

INTRODUCTION

Most of the sales happen because you hear something or someone buy and generally the word spreads through various medium. Would someone like to buy something that they haven't heard of till now in life? If at all they wish to buy, what could be the possible reasons and then would it be a product or a service. There is a pattern and a system one needs to understand how to sell and close a sale to anybody.

This book unfolds the secrets and tips to sell and close anybody that are time tested and proven. It basically starts with what your customer needs and how often they try to buy a product or a service. You will feel everything is under control, however let us look at certain scenarios that are common –

1. Whenever someone tells you that it is not enough if you just close a sale, but how to open and maintain a relationship.

2. At times you may wonder that while you have lots of customers, why to look for new ones.

3. You have an exclusive business that makes you feel you are the creator.

After reading the book, you will be able to understand the logic behind sales closures, from a salesman's perspective and from a customer's perspective. It is in5tended to be a guide that will serve the purpose of teaching you a thing or two about making the right choices for your products and services and is a guide for both the salesman and the customer. Well, everyone wants more, different and something new to show. For that matter, there is a lot of difference in the way customers perceive and understand buying anything. Simply, you wouldn't like to buy a comb the way you buy a hair gel.

The book identifies every need and scenario a salesman would go through and highlights possible solutions which will be of help in closing a sale. There are tips for everybody and will not concentrate on just one group of people. There is enough information to suit everyone and help them make a choice for themselves. The book is divided into various headings where each one will tell a separate story. It will ultimately help everyone in their pursuit to buy and sell products and services that will prove to be extremely useful.

The book will give you a glimpse of what it takes to both retain a customer and cause him or her to bring in more. Imagine having a number of customers who are all willing to bring in newer ones that are just as interested in buying your product or service. Will that not be good? It will completely turn your business around and you will have a good business. This book will try and tell you the secrets of finding new customers and also increasing your business potential. There are many people who wish to increase their customer base and this is easy to do if you follow the steps and techniques mentioned in this book.

How many people have you met lately?

To understand what needs to be sold and how to sell it, it is obvious that you need to get the pulse and what is the flavor of the season. People love to spread word about something that they buy and that word is precious. They will speak about something that has caught their fancy and others will try and copy them just to remain with the trend that is popular for the season.

So as a company looking to improve sales, there can be a million things to consider when you decide to sell a product. You cannot simply assume your customer will like something just by looking at a past trend. You need to understand what will please your customers and what it will take for them to buy your product or service. You cannot sell sweaters in summer and should wait until the rainy season to have your products sold.

Similarly, you need to make sure that people are ready to buy what you offer to them and more importantly, whether your upgraded product will be a hit amongst the existing customers. You must do your market research and for this, you need to take the right steps. You must understand how to persuade customers and convert them into complete buyers. You must take measures to help them make a choice for themselves. You need to tell them how you are bothered about them long after they have made their purchase.

Everything will count when you wish to make new customers and try and retain the old ones. As was already mentioned, this may consist lot of factors ranging from climatic conditions, buying behavior, economic conditions, trends and above all customer's interest levels which will be the most important criteria to consider as you will have to bear in mind their likes and dislikes to cater to them appropriately. This book covers details pertaining to the ways in which you can understand customer requirements, moods and what information you should seek when you try to gather information related to close your sale.

I want to thank you for purchasing this book and hope you will learn something new and interesting from it!

CHAPTER 1

YOU WIN WHEN YOU LOSE

Scenario 1: A team that won all the games and reached the final every season for the last six years. They definitely feel proud about the feat since no other team has that unique record. The other side of the story is that they failed to win in the finals every time they reached.

Scenario 2: After a 1000 failed attempts a scientist feels no motivation and reason to attempt once more. So he gives up, failing to realize how close he was and what else he achieved during the 1000 attempts.

Now you may wonder if there is anything in common in these scenarios and wonder as to why it is being cited here. Well, look closer and examine both the cases. You will understand that there is something common amongst them only if you pay keen attention to it.

You might have to make use of your skills to find the common ground and know exactly what connects these two scenarios. There is something that differentiates the two on the basis of their thinking. It is a little detail that is helping one and causing the other to suffer. This very thought might be the reason for your failure and for this, it is best that you figure it out for yourself. But if you haven't yet figured it out, then read on.

The common factor

A common factor that can be analyzed in both the scenarios is the recipe of 'secret for winning'. Most of the times, you may view failures as bad experiences and something that you do not want to think when you want your life to start on a positive note. In the process, if it is not happening you tend to give up in the moment when that extra mile could have been crossed to feel the magical moment.

Now the simple answer to all this is 'how to win' when you lose. Is there any kind of analysis you have to do, do you need to document your efforts or do you need to make more attempts crossing 1000 and continue. It might be tough at first to grapple with a loss. It is only human to feel down when faced with losses and adversities. But what will help is to stay positive and cut down on the negative as much as possible.

In the examples, the team that kept losing did not bother about losing in the finals and kept going at it. They saw the positive in the situation and concentrated on their record breaking run. They wished to continue pursuing their record and making it their trademark. The scientist however did not wish to make use of the information that he managed to amass during his 1000 attempts. He should have seen it as his positive and continued to do his research. Now let us say the team that reaches the finals will one day win the tournament. That will add a feather to their cap and they will be proud of winning it finally along with having the record of appearing in most finals.

Similarly, the scientist would have finally succeeded and along with success, he would have had a lot of theory and scientific backings to prove his final findings. The scientist lost out on all his opportunities because he chose to overlook the positives in his situation. There were high possibilities that he would have cracked the puzzle on his next attempt but he gave up without thinking of the consequences. This can be the decider between winning and losing and something that you need to consider before you give up on something.

So no matter what the consequences, it is always important to continue on with something regardless of whether or not it helps in proving to be a success. You will learn many things along the way and those things will be much more valuable than your final success. In sales, you must concentrate on winning the hearts of the customer more than looking at what they will ultimately buy from you. When you have many customers they will obviously bring others with them and that will finally help you increase your business. So no matter how many losses you face, you need to remain positive and try and make the most of the situation.

The Secret of converting your loss to a win

You think that analyzing a lost opportunity or losing a sale is not a topic that needs to be delved into. Certain times, you feel that you are already doing it in your way, what else needs to be analyzed. And the other factors that prompt you not to look at the pattern of losing is because of the costs, people involved and general beliefs everyone has. It is universally thought to be a waste of time to think about the losses. When a person has lost something then what is the point of looking at it as it will only make things worse. But why can't people look at it from the perspective that there can be a lot of positives in the losses as well. Just like how the win would have caused you to look into it for success, it is also important for you to look into your losing situation to convert it into a win. But for this, you need to adopt a certain method and technique and cannot go about it the wrong way. There should be a standard technique that you can adopt for all your analysis.

How can you go about analyzing your losses if you don't know what to look in it? You might only get discouraged to do so and change your mind over it. To prevent this, you need to try and remain positive when you analyze your losses and do the best that you can to convert your loss into a win. To help you in the process, look at the method you may adopt to understand what you need to do when you lose and convert it to a win.

The first logical step:

- Who are the customers, companies and entities you need to look at. This means that you do a thorough research of your customers and their needs. You cannot simply have an idea of who they are. You need to think before you act and do your research.

- Look at what your company or you wish to offer and the culture that prevails at your end. Look at all your offerings and what you offer to the end customer. Have a good knowledge of what is under your control before you decide to probe something that is not under your control.

- Create a thoroughly thought through questionnaire that you wish to seek answers about. You can write it down and put enough thought into it to seek all the right answers. It is important for you to understand that you need to keep the questions easy so that they understand what you are saying. They will not be ready to answer tough questions that they fail to understand. You need to start by looking into each of your problems and seek answers from customers to change your losses into wins.

- Start meeting your customers and choose the number strategically, or you may wish to look at a sale that you had lost very closely. Try and have a diverse group so that you have a chance to understand all their thoughts. It should consist of a diverse group so that you know what each one is thinking.

- Start talking to them and note down those important and valuable responses. Don't underestimate any of what the people have to say as everything is valuable. Don't dismiss any customer as you need to be in their good books for a very long time.

- Look and compare to what everyone said. Go through the manual several times to take into consideration every single aspect. It is easy to miss small things and so, remind yourself to go through the response several times. It is important that you stay as alert as possible when the customer is responding so that you capture their emotion and try and act upon it to help you serve them better next time.

- Analyze in your own way and shortlist the common reasons under certain headings. This means that there will be some things in common to what the people say and you need to subcategorize them. You will have a chance to understand what the common need is and cater to it in a better way. There will be a chance for you to understand the basic sentiment that everybody is resonating and take action on what needs to be done to fix it. By categorizing, you will have the chance to make the process easier for yourself.

- Recommend improvements if you work elsewhere and start implementing the changes wherever necessary. This is where you take action. You cannot rely too much on what you think went wrong alone and need to consider the end users opinion to try and incorporate as much change as possible to better your product or service.

- If you think you can go about this process in your own way then you can consider that as an option. You might have to come up with a method that you can see through till the end and have good results show up. If you choose complex processes then chances are you will not be able to finish it and so, try and keep it to a bare minimum. Don't think of any of it as a waste as you are doing this to help your business grow and you attain maximum sales.

Where you are and how you wish to see yourself

The moment you identify the reasons for failure and what you need to do to make that magic work, you are back to winning ways. It might sound a bit impossible but there are endless possibilities to what you can achieve if you put in a little thought and effort into it. If you feel like it is daunting then you need to think again. You cannot dismiss anything as being tough for you as it will only hold you back.

All you need to do is to keep working through the points mentioned earlier, for every attempt you make to close a sale or make something work for you. For this, you need to follow the steps just the way they were mentioned. Don't try to over think things or think for the customer. You must think for yourself and try and make your product or service as worthy as possible. You will be required to put in just as much hard work as is required by a company that is just starting out.

You cannot assume that things will fall into place just by you thinking about them. There will be many things to do and you must spring into action to get the various things readied to carry out the processes. If you turn lazy now, then rest assured, you will have problems in getting your work done. You need to find the strength to convert your loss into a win and for this you will have to work towards making progress. There is no possibility of you finding a short cut for this as there is no detours for success.

If you wish to see a change appear, then you will have to put in the effort for it. You need to try and make as much use of the information that you gather from your customers as possible. The differing opinions are what caused your problems to arise in the first place.

What you think might not match what others think. As was said earlier, you cannot think in lieu of the customer and need to stress on whatever will help your company make progress and you make maximum sale of your product. You will interestingly find new ways to attract the right kind of people, close all possible communication gaps, build knowledge irrespective of a win or a loss and be selective in choosing the right options.

Again, these right options will differ from company to company and you cannot generalize things. It is vital that you remain alert and keep your end goal in sight. In this case, the end goal is to try and get as many things done as possible for you to make enough sales and sell your products or services to as many people as possible and over turn your past losses into a roaring success!

The early warning system

One of the major strategic benefits of performing a win – loss analysis is that you will be able to create an early warning system if something is going out of control. An early warning system will help you to re-align your outcome and will help you to accomplish your goal. By going through the process of a win – loss analysis, you are able to document crucial information pertaining to the requirements of your customer.

The warning system is implemented for you to understand what might go wrong the next time you launch a product. It helps protect you against the damage by signaling o you that something is wrong and you can handle the situation in a better way. Imagine having an outside view of our business where there is an unbiased opinion towards what you are selling. It will help you remain alert and prevent a mishap from occurring.

This is the same system that most big companies employ as it helps them steer clear of making the same mistakes over and over again. The whole purpose of you having decided to conduct the survey was to turn your loss into a win and for this; you must use the information for as long as it will serve you rightfully. The early warning system will be applicable for all your products and services. It will be universally applicable and something that will assist you in predicting the future of how a sales pitch will go.

So when you create a product or a service and device a strategy to sell, you may choose to go with a plan with a sole idea of closing the sale. But it is not as we think; more often it happens that by the time you plan and go into the market, the choices and preferences would easily change due to a lot of factors. In such kind of scenarios, an early warning system will be of help in predicting what happens next, as you have already made analysis based on earlier loses.

It is vital that you not think of it as a fool proof way for you to predict something. It is just a warning system and will not do you a favor by fixing a problem. You need to read the signs in advance and try and take stock of the situation before it is too late again. For this, you need to have an eye out for all the various warnings and try and remain alert to pin point at them. Once you have access to the warning signs, you need to concentrate on whether are again repeating. If they are, then you need to try and act on them as fast as possible.

You cannot possibly try and predict something before it happens and for this, you must try and remain as positive as possible for the same to not repeat itself but if it does, you must take control and take up the right steps to curb the situation from getting out of hand. Again, you need to look for the positives and think of it as a warning sign that you are on treading on the wrong path and need to change your business to prevent the occurrence of any such problems in the future.

Customer retention and trends

In the first chapter of the book we looked at 3 scenarios, why we need more customers and why should you worry if your business doesn't have a competitor. Your job doesn't end if you just close one sale or if your luck strikes the right chord you may close one more. Losing is part of the game and without proper attention it may become a habit.

That might sound like a cliché but is the absolute truth. Imagine having to lose valuable customers just because you were not able to cater to them in the right way. That will be a tough situation to overcome as you will need immense strength and courage to re-approach a customer who has decided to walk away from you owing to you having been negligent. That is not the situation that is ideal for you to get yourself into, especially if you are a big company that sells many products. One word from a customer who is not satisfied and you could end up losing a whole lot of your business.

Remember that you need to diversify with your current customers in order to have them hooked on to your products. It is believed that most customers prefer brand loyalty which means that they will repeatedly buy something from the same brand if they are satisfied with one product. You may sell an umbrella to a customer in a rainy season or a summer season, but if you change your business to winter clothing it makes a lot of sense if you approach the same customer with a different product.

The actual success in sales is when you have a customer who repeatedly buys products or services from you and is comfortable is listening to anything you take to them. So try and diversify into parallel products that will win over the customer's hearts. It is not rocket science and you will not have to break your head over understanding what the customer is looking for. Chances are all the clues are right there and all you need to do is look into what the customer is interested in. say for example someone is buying dish liquid, then try and sell a scrubbing pad to the same customer by saying that the two will work well together and they will have better results by using them.

Trends relate to understanding the changing scenarios in a market, future behavior of the consumer and also what the competitor has to offer. Understanding trends also plays a crucial role in keeping pace with what your customer needs. Now let's say the person is interested in a parallel line of products and you don't have it. He or she might consider another company and their products and you might end up losing your customers to the other brand. This can be bad for your company as that customer might take with him or her others who are interested in parallel products as well.

So it is important to try and be at the top of your game and try and read your customers' minds. Remember that the parallel products will also help you attain new customers and your business will have a win win situation. You must not be bothered by what you think is the market for the parallel product. As long as it is something that your existing customers want, it is sure to keep you in business and increase your business.

CHAPTER 2

THE PERCENTAGE OF WINNING AND LOSING

In the previous chapter, we looked at all the things that you need to consider in order to turn around a bad situation and make it a good one. You must understand that there is a possibility for you to predict the number of customers that you can reach out to in order to sell your product. There are many theories that claim how most big companies know exactly who to target their audiences and how they plan on converting their temporary ones into loyal customers. For this, they are well versed with people's needs and desires. They also know to utilize their assets and this ultimately helps in making maximum sales of a product.

It all starts with the basic desire

In order to capture the basic desire of what someone wants is derived by having a marketing strategy in place to identify and sell a product or service. The best strategy is often knitted around the resources that are available with you. Depending on whether you have a lot of less, you need to go as per your budget. If you have only a few resources to employ, you will have to plan it out strategically and decide on what can be employed and where.

It is essential that you remain as intelligent and alert as possible and cut down on unnecessary wastage of precious resources. If you have a lot of resources at your disposal, you will still need to plan it out as it is essential for you to make the most of what you have. Some people go about it without a basic plan and end up wasting whatever is available to them. You will have to first take stock of everything that you have and then decide on what you will use and what you can save for later. You will need resources to conduct market research on the type of audience that is fit for your product and also the target customers.

You also need it for the research and development of the product that you wish to customize for your audience. All in all, you must be prepared with the right plan and the correct amount of resources to help you zero in on a product or service that will help make it easy for you to sell and for the customer to buy.

Imagine if you identified that your market needs high end flashy stuff with premium and elite tags and if you have the resources you may think of getting into it in a flash of a second. But if you don't have the resources you may wait or borrow to make it happen. Both cases you may end up in a risk of cash trapped situations if you have not understood the game properly. So the key is to follow a course of action that is befitting of a customer's wants. You will only be as good as your resource utilization. So try and make the best of the money, men and material resources that you have and use it to help you in your mission to understand and cater to the right type of audience.

So what do you do?

You should identify a market strategy that revolves around the buying habits of your customers and what you are planning to sell them. It is easily understood that there is a difference between selling a pen and selling a house. You need to understand the various situations and more importantly the details of the product or service that you are trying to sell.

You need to put yourself in place of the customer and analyze the situation. There should be no doubts in your mind in terms of who to sell it to. Everything should be clearly laid down and you must know who will take a fancy to what. Once you have sole your product to a particular customer, he or she will become your target again. This is because when you first buy, your reasoning as a customer is totally different from the next time you buy.

So, like it's said earlier in this book, that it is much easier to sell it to an existing customer than to sell it to someone totally new. If you have managed to get someone to come and buy your product then it is also possible for you to get them to buy more. This is easier than running after others who may or may not show an interest in what you are selling to them. It is not just easy but also a safe option as you can be rest assured of having a certain number of people coming back to you for their product and service needs.

Do some more research on your existing customers and find out what made them buy and the different situations that made them buy. Find out if you were good at doing something that attracted them in the first place and if that same tactic can be used again to make your customers stay. Remember that a happy person is like to shop with lots of excitement and chooses anything with lots of cheers and positivity. And if someone is unhappy the outcome is expected that they usually shop in a very dejected way. And an intelligent customer always tries to shop with logic and applies lots of math, calculations and reasoning.

So you need to do a thorough research on whether or not you are able to use something on someone again and make them remain loyal to your products or service. Finally, you need to make sure you also try and find new customers but not make it a top priority. Your top priority should be your current customers alone and attracting new customers can be your second priority.

The percentile method – designed to win

As was said in the beginning of the chapter, big companies make use of tactics that help them convert "maybe" customers into loyal ones. They will have knowledge on what it takes to retain a customer and cause them to remain loyal. For this, they may make use of the percentile system to help them decide on the exact numbers and convert tentative customers into sure shot ones. In this segment, we will throw some light on this topic and help you in understanding the % method better.

You should be able to work out a method that focuses more on winning and understanding situations where you may lose. The % mentioned below is a range chosen from the buyer's perspective and are taken in a broad range.

CHAPTER 3

TYPE 1: A CUSTOMER WHO IS 80% TO 90% LIKELY TO BUY:

Your customer in this case, ideally will buy irrespective of any situation as long as you have a product or service that is within their reasoning. These customers think rationally and are generally positive towards any decision they take in their life, be it for shopping or in anything else. They are firm headed and know exactly what they want from a product or a service. They do not panic and will have a perfect control on their lives in any kind of situation including financial control. They exactly know what is in the kitty and how much balance is left on the plastic card way ahead. They will be your customers who will give you repeat business. This will make them extremely predictable and the kind of audience that will help you make great headway in your business. These are the exact type of people that you need to retain in order to have a consistent supply and demand system in place. It might not be a bad idea to try your best to please these types of customers as they will only respond positively to whatever that you do for them. They will also value your efforts and try and remain as loyal to you to help the system remain in flow.

These types of customers view purchases as investments and also have the tendency of cutting down purchases if the money flow is curtailed. They don't feel stressed while shopping as they have a plan in place even before they start shopping. So the idea is for you to identify when they will decide to curb themselves and try and sell them something that will change their mind. As was mentioned, they will not negate anything that you suggest as long as it is in their best interests. They will only respond positively to the changes that you propose and once everything is back to normal they will start to revert back to their old buying habits.

What attracts them?

These types of customers plan way ahead of any season or occasion that comes by. For them, if an offer cites that on your second visit you will be able to save 30% on your purchase, they will buy it with convenience as they are sure of getting there the next time. These people will try and look into future prospects and decide on what will suit them the most. They will not hesitate in choosing you if you are offering them something that will work to their advantage. If they are buying crockery items for their kitchen and you offer them an apron at a discounted price, they would buy it as they don't wish to come again to buy it. They will make extremely smart choices for themselves as they will have full control over their minds and money. They are generally not unhappy if they don't leap on the given offer, rather at times they start thinking what other essentials that could be stacked up in the kitchen. This is mostly because they will try and make the most of the opportunity and buy things at one go. This will help them stay clear of falling into sales traps where they might end up over spending. They will look at the best time to attack the market and their level best to make the maximum use of a sale or an offer. That is what makes them extremely smart and capable of making all the right decisions for themselves and their families.

They will look at the price as a second option before they decide to buy something. And usually they are not upset if you try to sell them something and they don't get you wrong. They take everything as a learning experience if they have made a wrong move in buying something. So you need to hold on to these and push your luck with as many products and services as possible. You must have the capacity to change their minds and get them to agree with you. Once you win over their trust they will often listen to your advice and take into consideration the offer that you make to them. In the long run, these customers will help you turn your business into a roaring success and it is for these that you have to be grateful to the most.

How to sell more to these customers?

a. The moment they decide to buy: This is the time you have to identify and make them that offer of selling the apron. They will use words which you may easily understand like, "I am buying crockery for my home, and since I am around I am thinking what else would be interesting to look at". If I buy this, I wish to settle the bill once and for all and don't need to really take my money out and in again. This is the prime time for you to sell to them all the things that will go with their choice of shopping. It is important that you identify each and everything that will complement their first choice of product and show them how useful it will be to buy complimentary products. You can get into a demonstration mode to drive your point home and show them that they made the right choices in terms of the products that they chose to buy for themselves.

b. After they buy: Make sure that you don't makc too many offers at the same time after the purchase is over. Just because they heard you, it doesn't mean that they would buy it whenever you offer a product or service to them. They are less likely to buy in this case. You need to be extra careful with them as they will be your strong repeat customers and forcing them to buy immediately would make them think twice. So reserve anything that you wish to sell to them for the next time. If there is something that will tie together everything that they already bought then try and serve it to them. They might like your suggestion and give in. but this cannot be repeated time and again and there needs to be a limit on how many times you pull this trick. It might work just once or twice on them and not anymore. So be careful to not use this trick on the same repeat customer for more than twice or thrice and then move on to the next tactic.

c. When they buy and while they use it: If you are likely to contact them, you have to definitely know their preferred timings and mode of communication. They are customers who will experience every product or service they buy and wouldn't like to get distracted for any reason. So check out an ideal time if you are planning to sell an upgrade or suggest a different product immediately. For this, you need to keep track of their buying records. If you think a customer has been using a product for a year and the warranty is about to run out then you can get them on call and tell them about the upgraded product. With time, you will know exactly when to contact them again to sell them another product. You must remember that these customers might not return to buy just one thing and for this purpose, you need to have several items readied. You can again sell stuff in bulk to them and they will only be thankful to you.

d. While they are using it: Depending upon what they bought and how they are using it you may either suggest an upgrade or a new product or service to them. You have a 50-50 chance of them buying it as it depends on how they are experiencing the current product that is bought by them. For this, you must always offer good quality products to your repeat customers. It should be something that will make them happy and return to buy a new model or the same one as it helped them avail good service.

e. Sometime later: These customers are likely to be your repeat customers and some for life long. If you contact them after a few months or in some cases years, they would still not hesitate to confirm a sale and pay a token amount and may be buy later not to lose on the offer. So try and maintain as many records of repeat and loyal customers as possible in order to experience good sales. You can digitize all your records and maintain them for a long time. Remember that your 80% to 90% customers are your prime target and you must do all that it takes to keep them happy and retain them for the longest periods of time.

CHAPTER 4

TYPE 2: A CUSTOMER WHO IS 60% TO 70% LIKELY TO BUY:

In the previous segment, we looked at easy customers who will be easy to manage given how organized they are. It is always an easy task to persuade someone interested in buying something to buy another thing but what happens if someone is not so interested? Do the tactics change? Well, let us find out.

The second type of customers that we are looking at is those that are 60% to 70% likely to buy something from you. They are those that might not be too interested in your products as in the case of the 80 to 90%. Those will be extremely grateful to suggestions as they will have an open mind but the same cannot be said about the people in this category. Although it is hard to classify your general crowd percentage wise, doing so will only help you make the most of your business. You might have to make use of a little wit and observe your customers to understand who falls into which category. People in this particular category might be simply look around and have a few things in their basket.

These customers may buy what you try to sell, but are not always happy as in the case of 80-90%. They carry some stress and are emotional towards certain aspects in life that reflects in their buying behavior as well. They are logical but have a different reasoning when it comes to buying and will not be as free or open minded as the 80 to 90% customers. They will value their resources better and might not walk in being as organized or have a clear idea of what they want or what will work best for them at your store.

These customers are likely to buy from you if you keep them comfortable and not trouble them too much by suggesting too many things at one time. You need to give them their space and let them pick up things for themselves before you start bombarding them with suggestions. Their confidence levels will be low compared to the 80-90% type of customers and they are likely to buy stuff from you based on their current state of mind as they will not be confident in paying for too many things at once.

They will think twice and there is a lot that goes through their mind, before they hit the decision button of buying and until then, they might simply be walking around looking at everything that you put on offer to them. . This behavior may at times lead them to stress and anxiety and they end up in not buying anything as they will not be able to make up their mind on any one type of thing. They feel today is not the best day and probably someday it will be fine and they will have the chance to make a quicker and better decision for themselves.

There might be discrepancies in terms of the color or the pattern on a product or a slight difference between two or more services that you offer. All of it will cause them to get confused and they will decide to wait it out until they have a clear mind to buy something from you. Due to this, they relate this inability of choosing towards the price of a product.

The first purchase plays an important role and is linked towards their future purchases from you. Imagine if the initial purchase keeps them very excited then they will decide to buy a lot from you in the future. And then they also could be your repeat customers and at times lifelong customers too. But for this to happen, you need to show them products that will instantly catch their fancy and more importantly, fit into their budget. If they do not have the budget for what you show to them then they will immediately term you as being "too expensive" and avoid coming to you in the future. That is not something that you want and for this, you should be able to tell what the customer might be interested in and how much they might be ready to shell out. But do not ask them blatantly and try to look at the products that they are choosing and the price range of each of those products.

These types of customers also seek a lot of advice from near and dear ones. They will find it hard to confirm for themselves that their choice in life is extraordinary and that they made a unique choice. Instead, they may look at what the herd has to say and tend to go with it. They will look at what their family members have bought and use it to see if it is worth buying. So it will help to ask them if they have read about any of these products or someone that they know is using it so that you can try and sell them the very same product as they will be interested in buying the same. And finally these types of customers are people who think that fate has a cruel role to play on them and that is why they are unable to buy anything with ease. They will not be able to instantly decide on something and think that their fate is dictating their buying tendencies. They will remain tied to this idea and wonder if your shop is not right for them.

What attracts them?

If there is a timer set to the offer they may feel a lot stressed and will not be in a position to make the right choice. You cannot possibly stress them out by saying this offer ends today or tomorrow as they will feel the pressure and decide to run out of your store and not come back. They would need a lot of time to think before they make the right choice. While offers may excite them there should be enough time for them to choose the product which has that offer. So tell them about an offer that is valid until a month or more. That is the right time for them to make the choice for themselves.

If you tell them about offers that are going to end soon, then they will not buy the product. This is the exact opposite behavior that the 80 to 90 % customers showcase. Those will be excited about getting something within the offer period and it will help them return back during times of offers and sales. So this tactic needs to be changed when it comes to the 60 to 70% buyers and you need to make sure that you understand which customer is in what range.

Similarly, it will also affect them adversely if you say that there are limited pieces of whatever that they are trying to buy. So if you pitch a sale for them saying that there are only two or three left to buy in the offer, they may not be keen to buy as they apply logic and decision making that takes time. You need to have offers for them that may last for a few days or at times even months and also a sticker that says the number of people purchased the product or service. They don't mind if you send them information about the same product a few times as they would need enough time before they decide to buy.

As was mentioned earlier, they tend to follow the herd and if they see that many people have already bought something then they will also decide to buy the same thing. They will be extremely happy if you say that around 10 or 15 people bought this today as this offer is good and this product is also very good and they will immediately pick it up for themselves. They will not hesitate thinking whether the product is worthy as they will be influenced by the choice that others have made for themselves. But remember to be honest and only quote the number of people that have actually bought the product from you or if you have valid statistics that claim how many are being sold all around and also show them these reports for them to believe you better.

They are cool when it comes to promoting you are your product referring to their friends. Irrespective of the purchase being made, they will advocates of your product or service if they really like what they bought from you. So you need to keep them happy and show them that your products are great to buy and will deliver on quality and price. They will not mind broadcasting about your product even if they have not purchased something big and might speak of something else that they saw in your store. If this information falls on the ears of the 80 to 90% customers then they will help turn into your repeat customers and you will be able to make quite a lot of business thanks to these 60 to 70% people.

How to sell more to these customers?

a. The moment they decide to buy: You have to be very cautious and careful that enough time is given to them when they decide to buy something from you. They come with a clear mind regarding what to buy and they are not really keen on how much money they wish to spend. They will generally have only a limited amount and might not be interested in splurging on something that they are not confident in buying. They might not be up for an unlimited budget; rather they would be keen on what is a permissible limit for them to buy something. If you try to offer them something when they decide to buy, make sure they relate to it in the course of action. Don't run to them at the last minute and say this product will work well with what you buy. That tactic might work on the previous type of customers but not here. If you wish to make a deal with them and close the sale then give them enough time to think about all the products that you are offering to them and try not to give them something at the last minute.

b. After they buy: Now that they have decided and bought it from you, they feel more comfortable and are keen to spread the good word around. This time around, if you make an offer they are more likely to buy it from you probably as a combo offer. At the same time, you have to make sure that the offer that is being made should not have any hidden agendas or should not be time bound. This is best done when they come the second or third time. Don't try to do this the first time as they might wonder if you have some hidden motive. These people will think twice for everything and that is something you must try and work around. When you tell them that you are willing to offer them something at a discounted rate along with something that they have already bought then they will be more than willing to oblige and pick up the other product or products from your store as well.

c. When they buy and while they use it: Again, this is a good time to make a combo offer or a new offer to this buyer as they feel relaxed after making the purchase decision. Just that, you should not make them feel urgent to buy the product or service as they just made one. The offer which you make essentially need not be related to their original purchase as they tend to view the second purchase as a new one. The take away point for this type of customer is that while they wait to receive their purchase, you may talk to them about the benefits and if possible certain coupons on their next purchase. They feel attracted and comfortable to make the next purchase. You can tell them about this during the course of their purchase or wait for them to be done with their current purchase. The advantage of telling them about it all throughout their shopping is that they will return back soon enough to redeem the coupons that you give them and might come back within the same week as the initial purchase. If you give them coupons at the last minute then they might not remember well enough and might not come back as early to use these coupons and arriving just before they expire will again cause them to stress out.

d. While they are using it: At this point of time, they do not have any fear whatsoever about what the whole world thinks or how many people really use it. They feel elated and are part of what they have just bought. Freebies with a surprise are something which you can make these customers extremely happy. So make a point that while they have bought their original purchase, you add certain freebies and discount coupons prompting them for their next purchase. This freebie need not always be extremely valuable price wise but if it is something that will complement what they are purchasing then they will be extremely happy. This is the same as the 80 to 90% people looking for complimentary products to buy except that these people will be looking to get it for free. So say they buy themselves some dog food. You can offer a nice dog collar or dollar to them and they will be extremely happy with the freebie. They will decide to buy the same from you every time just to check for a freebie.

e. Sometime later after first purchase: Since they are basically emotional and have the tendency to have failed or stressed relationships they try to seek a bond elsewhere. At this point, if you tend to maintain a business relationship by keeping them posted on the latest offers, sending them a card related to seasons' greetings, they feel elated and on cloud nine. They start to relate to your emotionally and think that you are a great store and broadcast about you. This will again help you make new customers and they will be eager to establish the same type of relationship with you. And when they feel the time is right, they will buy one of the offers from the list you had sent earlier. So try and remain in their memory as much as possible and give them the opportunity to remember you whenever it is ideal for them to buy something new.

CHAPTER 5

TYPE 3: A CUSTOMER WHO IS 40% TO 50% LIKELY TO BUY:

In the previous segment we explored the mindset of the 60 to 70% type of customers and looked at how they might be interested in things if others take a fancy for it. Now, we will look at the mindset of those people that fall into the 40 to 50% category.

These people are said to be the type that probably have the most potential to convert but it is tricky to break into their psyche. They will not be fooled easily and will put thought into everything that they decide to buy.

These customers have certain traits of the two types explained above. They are confident, emotional, logical and excited. But they are not planned unlike Type 1 customers. They will not seem as organized and you can tell if they have come with an agenda or not. They do not have a start point and an end point and don't plan their day or sequence at all. They will prefer to walk around and have a look at every single thing in the store and walk at a snail pace as they will not feel the need to rush the process of shopping. They might also consider it as being a very therapeutic experience and wish to walk around the store to reel in a good experience. They are usually outspoken and are able to grab eye balls just at the word go. They can be a little loud and try and appear as though they have a knowledge on everything that is in the store. They are usually positive and fun loving people, hence they would like a lot of experiences that they would like to cherish and share. They will have no qualms in broadcasting about you and your store. They will be glad to speak out about the products that your store offers and what it is that makes yours unique. They will have a lot of connections in general and their word will be valuable to most of them. This will work to your advantage and you will have the chance to increase your customer base as also have a variety coming in and not just other 40 to 50% ones alone. They will love to have company and might always have a friend or relative accompanying them at the store. They will have a good time looking at everything and speaking about its best features. They will want to know every small detail of each and everything and have a logical conversation with their companion to analyze whether it is worth it to buy the product or not.

They do not feel any urgency of getting into things unless it is time. If you try to make them understand that the offer ends by tomorrow they don't see a reason or urgency behind it and will not rush to buy it. This is more like the type ii customers as they will forgo anything that will give them stress. Here they will not express any particular desire to buy things that are on offer, especially those that have limited stock or limited time to buy. They usually do not do anything on time unless they feel the urgency to do so. This can be slightly tricky as there is no one rule that will apply to the entire collection of customers in this range. The limited stock might work on some people and might not on others so it is tricky to tell as to what might have an effect on the customer and what might not. Through time, you will be able to tell the difference depending on the person's buying and shopping behavior. If a particular customer from this range is looking at products on offer that are about to go out then it is easy for you to understand what will work on them and if it is someone that is looking at products that are having a limited period 10% extra quantity then you will know that these people are looking for freebies and extras and that is their urgency. As was said earlier, they are people who like shopping and can go on for a long time. They do not search for a reason to choose and buy a product or service. They will just come with the idea of shopping and not any other type of agenda. They will prefer to do their research on the spot as opposed to coming in with an idea of what is the best deal to go in for. If you think they are missing company that they like to have then you can start walking around with them and converse as though you are also a fellow customer and try and get them to listen to your opinions while you agree with theirs.

What attracts them?

These customers might not be soft nuts to crack. They can be extremely smart and logical but in no position to rush their shopping like type I. these people will be more interested in the experience and if they find something interesting to buy then that will be like a reward for them.

While it is true that they really like to shop again and again, they wouldn't like to be dumped on to everything one time. They feel to buy one more now; they may miss out the time to shop for the next time. So if you are trying to make an offer to them on their existing purchase they are least likely to buy at this point of time. They will think of making a comeback for the product so that they can again indulge in shopping, which is their favorite activity. They will see no point in rushing towards making any sort of a purchase and will be less likely interested in rushing to do buy something. However, remember that they have less patience, if they want to buy something they would rather go to a place where it is readily available irrespective of offers or no offers and they would buy it right away. Most of the times they will not have the patience to wait till it is shipped and feel rather restless and incapable of waiting for a good offer to come by.

They would get attracted to anything that is easy to buy as in the process to buy. They wouldn't like to go through a painful process of buying something and if that happens they jump out of the queue and look for something else that will complement what they have. This is mainly because they will consider shopping their priority and not necessarily look for items that are useful. If something catches their eye then they will look into its features and decide to buy it. Anything that improves their personality and will keep them creatively occupied is what they will be interested to buy. They might not consider the price as much if they think that the product is from a good company and is adding value to their life. For these types of customers, it is ideal to place fancy things near the billing counter as they will be occupied with it and decide to buy something from there. They will take a fancy to anything that is nice and efficient and more importantly, well packed. They will value every little detail that has gone into making the product look good and it will help them remain satisfied with you and your store. They will look at the last counter as their treat and try and wait it out before hitting it. This will only make them look around more and you will have the chance to sell to them more and more things. Again, they might not buy everything from the last counter and wait for their next trip to do so. So try and limit the variety on the counter so that they are tempted to return back within a few days as they will see it as being an urgent need to pick up something that they have already taken a fancy to.

How to sell more to these customers?

a. The moment they decide to buy: There is no second thought at this point when they make the decision. And the buying goes beyond control if they are in the mood to buy. At this point, if you roll out offers that have 50% off on the second immediate purchase or buy one get one free. Again, these people are disorganized and won't have a plan. They will walk around the store without a single plan to stick to and will generally wish to pick things as and when they come across these as opposed to hitting their counter in advance. It will be easy for you to trick them into buying something if you place it at the last counter as they will feel the urgency to pick it up before they start billing. You can have a counter that looks quite fancy and capable of catching their attention from afar.

b. After they buy: You will not find them at all. This is mainly because they seek variety. They might be impatient in standing in lines and will wish to wander away. If they need anything they are likely to come back. If they come with their partner to shop, the moment they end the shopping they may tell their partner to handle the rest. They will think of hitting another store that sells similar products so that they can have a new shopping experience. They will not be hung up on shopping at just your store and the only thing that might make them come back is a nice place where you have stacked lots of interesting things that they can go through. So the idea of selling more to them at this point is a waste of time. You can instead focus on trying to keep in touch with them with the idea of getting them back and this time, you will have a better plan to deal with them.

c. When they buy and while they use it: If you offer them something better on the product or service they are likely to use, this is it they will take it just like that. If they have bought a holiday package, that originally had a 3 day stay and you tell them you could offer a free spa and an upgrade offer worth in terms of the experience, they would buy it. But it should be close to what they are looking for and ideally be within the price range that satisfies them. They will be highly interested in those things that excite them and less likely to buy things that are not exciting. If they are on a mission to buy just one sort of thing then try and call them to tell them about a parallel product that is quite useful with the thing that they bought. This will excite them and give them a chance to visit your store again and if they take a fancy o something else then you can try and turn them into repeat customers.

d. While they are using it: At this point of time, if you offer them discounted rates or coupons for their next purchase, they may not be too keen to have a look at what you have to offer. Instead, if they just bought a music player and the Bluetooth speakers are really attractive to go with, they may grab the offer. Anything that helps them to make the experience better, they would jump to it. So be ready with a few parallel products in mind. They will not be patient if you run to look for something and even if it is really useful even then they will not consider it as being something of value to them. You need to be prepared well in advance to offer them something unique so that you can immediately show it to them and have a chance to sell them the products at the earliest.

e. Sometime later: You have to be in touch with them or sending them information related to a wide variety of things. You never know, what they would like and how they would like to respond back. But they would surely buy it at some point, if it is better than the previous one the experience is going to be thrilling. So make sure you send them information on things that you are sure will excite them. They will come running to buy it as it will work to be an urgency for them to have the products. You must put in thought to send them a list of parallel products so that you can sell them as many things at one time. And even if they don't buy it during their visit they will surely come back for it the second time. The advantage of keeping in touch with all types of customers regardless of which category they fall in is that you will have a better chance at selling your products as you never know what will excite which type.

CHAPTER 6

TYPE 4: A CUSTOMER WHO IS 20% TO 30% LIKELY TO BUY:

By now we have looked at 3 types of customers and their shopping trends. Now, we will look at the next category of people which is the 20 to 30% likely ones. You must understand that there can be a wide range and that there will be a mixture of people at one time and there won't be an exclusive group walking in at one time. So you need to have your eyes peeled to look for the various types of people so that you can sell the right product or service to the right type of customer.

Now, we shift focus to the 20 to 30% group. This group of people will be just as interested in shopping and have no agenda. They will however resemble the type I in that they will be intelligent and logical in thinking about their buying decisions.

They also apply logic, but towards the negative side of analyzing things. You would never want a customer like them in your target list. They can be extremely tricky to interpret and you will have a tough time trying to make sense of what they are looking for. It will be tough for you to interpret their psyche as they might say one thing but do another. And they have this general feeling that some point in life, the whole world is going to be against them and this thinking is what will make them shop impulsively. They might not be in a position to make the right choice for themselves when they are buying impulsively and might take home everything that they do not need. But if they come with a motive then they will only buy those things that they really need. They do not know what and how much they need in life, be it money or possession of things. At times, they think they do not have anything even if they have money. They may also be obese and with less physical activity. They do not have anything in order and do not like to keep things in shape even if it is needed. So they will appear quite disturbed and not at all organized. You will be able to identify this type just by the way they walk and how disorganized their cart or basket will appear.

Most of the times, they do not shop and when they do it is called a 'shopping spree'. This is unlike normal people's spree and will include buying everything that is important at once whether there is any logic behind it or not. But if you try to fool them then they will be able to surmise it and will catch you red handed in the act. They will know exactly what they need to buy during most of their sprees but if you put in a little effort then will be able to sell them something that will interest them and they will buy it. They also carry this guilt of not buying anything for others and do not know where to stop buying for themselves. They will think of it as a mission to fill their carts with things that will make them happy and also get something with it that they can give to their loved one. Those things might cause them to be satisfied temporarily. This aspect they will not understand and think that they will be happy for a long time but realize that their happiness has ended by the time they have gone home with their product or service and immediately feel the need to buy something else of value.

What attracts them?

The first thing to find out is, if these kind of customers are buying anything for others than themselves. While it is easy to say and difficult to find out, but if you want that extraordinary sale to happen and your target of the month to be completed at one go – take a chance, play the role of a strategist thinker or a soothsayer and find out. And nothing like if you know what their hobbies are, because they are likely to shop more if it fits them and their tastes. It will excite them to have the option of buying something for themselves that will bring them satisfaction. It will give them joy to know that their interest has been taken care of and you are helping them with things that will be of great value to them. They will also be happy if you volunteer to walk around with them and hold their basket or push their cart as it will help them shop better. If they are obese and trying to manage everything at once then they will remain distracted and not be in a position to have a proper shopping experience.

If you make an offer to them that they are sure to use in the coming times, they become restless till they buy it. They get stressed, if they feel they are spending too much money on shopping at a particular time. You could try and speak to them about the offer and they may choose to buy it later as they feel someday they will possess it and that there is no need to hurry. The whole idea is to be on the same page as your customers and not worry them or psyche them out. They need to understand that you are emotionally supporting them and agree with their decisions. There is a reason why the customer is known as the king and you need to make sure you respect what they are saying. If you bombard them with too many things even if it is good things then they will start to feel anxious and walk away. You never know what a person's threshold might be and when they might trip. It is essential that you not decide to trip them as that might cause them to leave the store for good. These 20 to 30% types can be a big pain but you cannot decide to walk away from them as every single customer is valuable. You might have to put in a little extra effort to decipher these and keep them happy but it will be well worth it if you try and remain positive. Once you get into the customer's good books, you will be able to keep them happy for a long time. Anyway the main goal for you is to convert all your customers into repeat customers as it is easier to maintain them as opposed to looking for new ones. If 20 to 30% ones are causing you worry then it will not be worth it. You need to be grounded and firm headed in order to tackle them. If they get even a slight hint of you not being interested in showing them around or answering their questions then they will not hesitate from walking out. You need to show them some interest and make them believe what you say is true. As was mentioned earlier, it is best to always put yourself in the customer's shoes to understand what will please them and what will not. It will be easy for you to tell whether he or she is interested in your products or service if you interpret your behavior from their view point. You need not stress over the fact that these might not come back to you and try and make the most of their first visit. If you apply the techniques mentioned thus far then rest assured, you have full chances of getting your customers to coming back to you. You need to patiently apply each type and then wait for the fruits of your labor to ripen. With time, you will become wise and be in a great position to close any type of a sale to any type of customer.

How to sell more to these customers?

a. The moment they decide to buy: At this point, you will not be able to sell anything to them. They are not the rush type on looking at combo offers or coupons for the next buy. The only thing that they may be attracted to is, if their current purchase offers anything to their beloved or friends at a less price, they would look at it as it is a good chance for them to satisfy them. This will lessen their guilt to a large extent and they will be satisfied with their buy. They might also be interested in knowing if they can gift the coupon to someone that they know so that they can redeem it at the time of purchase. All of it will ultimately help them remain satisfied with their current trip and might prompt them to return back to your store for their next "spree".

b. After they buy: This is a good time to offer them more, or give them additional benefits on their current purchase. They would look at the value of gifting it to their beloved or friends on something they just bought. For this, you can add in something at the last minute as a surprise. It will satisfy them to know that they have shopped to their heart's content and also had a chance to buy something for their near ones. Such a situation is what they will be on the lookout for and you will have the chance to satisfy them. if you think you need to make a little profit out of it then you can choose things like an extra pack of the same thing can be bought for just a few dollars more. This will make them happy as they will have the chance to give to their loved ones the same thing that they bought for themselves. They will not have to look for anything different and will get what they want without having to walk around anymore.

c. When they buy and while they use it: After they buy it and while they are likely to use it, you may offer them something more. They would surely look at the offer. If they are booked on a plane for an economy class and receive a mail for an upgrade to business class if booked for two, they are likely to buy it. This will help them satisfy the other person as well. They will feel good about the offer and be in a good position to give the nod. Here, they anyway have to buy the one ticket and if they have the chance to make a profit just by booking one more seat and take along a dear one then they will not hesitate from doing it.

d. While they are using it: If they feel comfortable and the offer is related to what they are currently using then they would go for it. If they just bought a laptop and a set of HD movies that could be played on it are in for a discounted price they are likely to buy it. They might also decide to keep some of the movies and gift the rest. It is vital that you interpret their mind in a way that helps you conduct your business. You will be able to show them that you are interested in helping them make the most of their purchases and spree and you respect their time and effort. If you think it will work for you to give away a box set of DVD's at a further discounted price then do not hesitate as they are sure to take up your offer. As was said earlier, if you do not wish for fussy customers to be your repeat customers then try and make the most of their first visit so that you do not have to deal with them repeatedly and cause yourself a headache.

e. Sometime later: Irrespective of whether they buy it or not, they would like to keep themselves informed about what is happening. Since they always think about it, they would buy it sometime or later and so, don't take them off the list just because you think they are least likely to buy something from you. No customer is any less valuable than the other. You cannot dismiss them off thinking they are fussy. Even if they will not return as often, they might come in once in a while and buy a lot of things in bulk. This will only help you remain satisfied and them loyal. So send out tailor made offers to these people so that they are tempted to drop by and buy whatever that is catching their fancy.

CHAPTER 7

TYPE 5: A CUSTOMER WHO IS 0% LIKELY TO BUY:

Unlike the previous types, this is something to be informed about and not to feel guilty about. They are full of agony and you know they buy. And the minute they buy, they feel as if they own you or your place. They have problem with everything they come across in life. They feel the whole world is corrupt and anything that tries to grab their attention, they feel it is a plan to pull them in a whirlpool. They will think it is a conspiracy and you are in on it. Even if they purchase something of very little value they will wonder if you tried to cheat them. They will then and there declare their disinterest in visiting you again and you need not worry about them. They might act like they did you a favor by buying something from you and you can simply smile and nod at them. They will get going in no time and you will forget about them in even lesser time.

You can't do anything about customers of these types but be careful about how to deal with them. You don't need to feel bad that you are not able to sell anything to them or you missed your target because of not selling to them. You must understand that even if you tried your best then they will not be in a position to agree with your perspective and will only do what they think is right. Instead of wasting your time with them, you may look at the other types and focus your energy on reaching your targets. Remember that you need to cut down on your negatives and up your positives. If you spend too much time delving into the negatives alone then you will have a problem making progress. So don't be bothered by people that are worthless and concentrate on those that are well worth retaining and catering.

If you have salesman who are assigned with the task of catering to the customers then you need to train them to identify and apply the different techniques depending on the category of the customer. If they are not well versed in it then you might have trouble retaining and converting your customers. Make sure you conduct regular sessions and teach them how they can close a deal.

You can make use of CCTV cameras and observe customer behavior. This will make it easier for you to know who is what sort of a customer. You can also show the footage to the salesmen and get them to identify them. But you need to be discreet about it as most people don't like to be observed. They will feel complexed about it and if they find out you are observing them then they might not return. If you want you can inform them in advance about it so that they are not taken by surprise at the sight of cameras glaring at them.

If you have a range of premium products on offer then the 80 to 90% customers are your target, if you wish to sell goods that are popular then you can sell it to the 60 to 70% crowd. If you deal in goods that are unique and exciting then those will suit the 40 to 50% and if there are freebies or things of extra value on offer then the 30 to 40% will take fancy. But there is probably nothing that will satisfy the 0% types and you need not plan anything for them as it will be a waste.

CONCLUSION

I want to thank you once again for downloading this book and hope that you found it informative.

You may need to apply different strategy to different people at different places. At times your strategy of thinking only to close a sale and get the customer agree to buy could work out. But at the same time, it is not good to force the customer to buy something just for the heck of it. While your intention is to make the customer buy what you sell, it should be in a way they are comfortable with or understand the need better. Put yourself in their situation and analyze the scenario. Would you like it if someone tried to sell you something that is of no use to you? You will try and avoid that company in the future as well because of your bad experience. Similarly, you must understand your customer base and their needs in order to sell the right product to the right person. This is where most people go wrong and end up upsetting people by trying to push their product to uninterested personnel.

One of the best techniques for closing could be to hear what the customer has to say. You should not talk all the time, by doing so you may miss out on certain key points which the customer has in their mind. And when you tend to listen to them, it builds a level of curiosity in them and you have a bright chance that will get inclined towards your sale. You need to ask something and then wait for him or her to finish completely. Some people have the habit of putting their thoughts in which will cause the customer to forget about the things that they had in mind. You need to be supportive and nod your head instead of trying to speak with them or for them.

Emotions play a crucial role in closing a sale. You need to check out the level of emotions the other person carries, while you are conversing with them. Try to always be on the positive side of their emotions which will allow you to close the sale in much effective manner. Again, nod your head and smile when they make an emotional point. Try and connect with them in such a way that they feel as though you relate to their problems or issues and are genuinely interested in helping them out. There needs to be a balance of emotional and logical actions when it comes to persuading a person to buy what you wish to sell to them. The two of you must develop a rapport which will help them trust you. Always put yourself in the customer's shoes to understand their needs and wants. If you pretend like you are clueless about what they are saying then they will be discouraged to speak out the truth. Similarly, if you say something contradicting to their thoughts just to sell your item then you will again end up discouraging them. All of it will ultimately result in the customer not interested in your product and might simply decide to play along.

And finally closing essentially doesn't mean the sale happened today. A multi-million dollar sale could take three years to complete and realize the value and money. So don't try and rush something and do your best to remain as positive as possible. If it is meant to happen then it will happen. You need not worry about it if you have done all the right things. It might take some time for the customer to be ready to shell out a lot of money but it will happen for sure if you have adopted all the right techniques to close your sale.

The most essential part is to maintain a relationship with your customer thinking long term and always try to find ways to close the deal effectively by using proven secrets and tips as mentioned in this book. Once you understand the various types of customers you come across and how to sell them, you have mastered the art of making them say 'yes' and make them say yes repeatedly. Once you garner confidence, you will be able to sell more and more of your product to many more customers and whether you are a salesman or a company dealing in the products, nobody will be able to stop you from making positive progress.

FREE BONUS VIDEO

INSPIRATIONAL SALES VIDEO MUST WATCH BY SALES TRAINING EXPERT GRANT CARDONE

Bonus Video: https://www.youtube.com/watch?v=DnKJDlaPI2c

Checkout My Other Books

http://www.amazon.com/Job-Interview-Techniques-Negotiating-Persuasion-ebook/dp/B00PFFK7EE/ref=sr_1_4?s=digital-text&ie=UTF8&qid=1430018739&sr=1-4&keywords=job+interview

http://www.amazon.com/Negotiating-Strategies-Techniques-Influencing-Negotiation-ebook/dp/B00SOK8ODI/ref=sr_1_1?s=digital-text&ie=UTF8&qid=1430018775&sr=1-1&keywords=negotiating

www.ingramcontent.com/pod-product-compliance
Lightning Source LLC
Chambersburg PA
CBHW070958180526
45168CB00003B/1200